SANTORINI
THE PREHISTORIC CITY OF AKROTERI

CHRISTOS G. DOUMAS
Ph. D. University of London
Ephor of Antiquities

ATHENS

EDITIONS HANNIBAL

Cover plate (on the front)
Akroteri
The wall-painting of the Boxing Children trom Room B1.

Cover plate (on the back)
Akroteri
The Fisherman Fresco which decorated the north-eastern corner of Room 5 in the West House.

Translated by
ALEXANDRA DOUMAS

Photographs by
HANNIBAL

Supervision of printer's proofs
ELEFTHERIA KONDYLAKI

Colour reproductions
CHRISTOS ANTONIADES

Phototypeset by
FOTRON A.S.

Printed by
EKTYPOTIKE

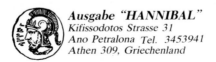

Ausgabe "HANNIBAL"
Kifissodotos Strasse 31
Ano Petralona Tel. 3453941
Athen 309, Griechenland

SANTORINI
THE PREHISTORIC CITY OF AKROTERI

Diamond set on the ring of Santorini, Phera, the island's capital, reflects man's dramatic struggle to be reconciled with the elements of nature. It simultaneously demonstrates his attempt to beautify this struggle. For it is not only Phera's position on the very rim (phrydhi) of the caldera which makes it unique in the Aegean. It is also its architecture which reveals the sensitivity and creative imagination of a simple people. With the cheap materials readily available in abundance, the folk builder has managed to solve all problems, — of shelter, social and economic — creating at the same time masterpieces of his craft (ill. 1, 5). Examples of folk architecture also are the picturesque little churches, modest offerings of the humble believers of Santorini. Folk artisans also were those who adorned the church interiors with carved wooden altar screens (templa) and icons. Some of these works rank among the rare creations of our folk art (ill. 6 - 8.).

Santorini owes its birth to its volcanicity. Its entire fate, the happiness or misery of its inhabitants, is intimately bound to the volcano. This, with its lavas, gave birth to Santorini, this enlarged it, this subsequently shattered it into bits. One can follow the whole of this dramatic process when ascending the 600 or so steps from the old harbour (Ormos) to Phera (ill. 2, 4). Surrounded by lavas of black and red and ash, one feels at certain moments, as one climbs up, as if one is in the very bowels of the earth and only the presence of the mules and donkeys, the sympathetic mode of transport in this case, brings one back to reality.

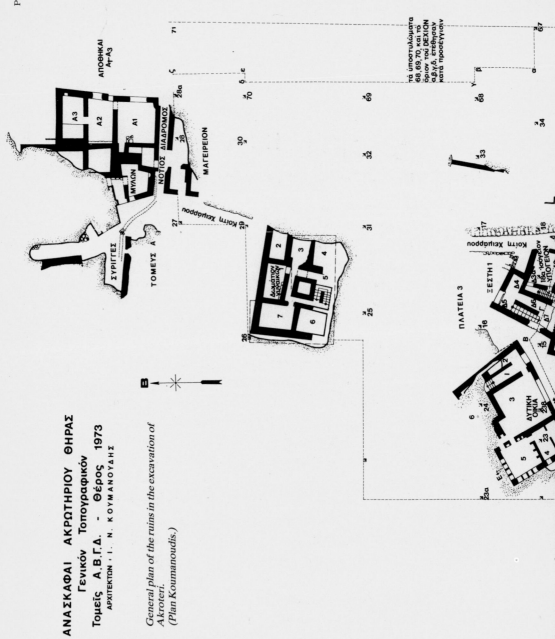

ΑΝΑΣΚΑΦΑΙ ΑΚΡΩΤΗΡΙΟΥ ΘΗΡΑΣ
Γενικόν Τοπογραφικόν
Τομείς Α.Β.Γ.Δ. - Θέρος 1973
ΑΡΧΙΤΕΚΤΩΝ · Ι. Ν. ΚΟΥΜΑΝΟΥΔΗΣ

*General plan of the ruins in the excavation of
Akroteri.*
(Plan Koumanoudis.)

The island's economy is also connected with the volcano. The thick strata of volcanic ash do not merely constitute the shroud which buried Santorini deep within the earth. They comprise its fertile soil which favours all kinds of cultivation with especial emphasis on viticulture (ill. 9). These layers are also an important source of wealth themselves for they are exported as mined material. Pozzuolana (Therian earth) was used by the engineer of the Suez Canal, Ferdinand de Lesseps, to insulate its walls in 1866. From then until now Santorini has, uninterruptedly, supplied the world with this material. Millions of tons of pozzuolana are exported annually from the island's quarries for use in the cement industry and as insulating material in various constructions (ill. 3).

These layers of pozzuolana, which sometimes exceed 30 metres in thickness, were created after a mighty eruption of the volcano which occurred in about 1500 B.C. According to the experts on the island's geology, Santorini was round in shape prior to this eruption and its volcanic cone was approximately 1800 metres above sea level. Upon this circular isle lived the prehistoric inhabitants from at least the middle of the third millennium B.C. as archaeological research has verified. Up until about the middle of the second millennium B.C. (circa 1600) the inhabitants of Santorini followed the culture which flourished throughout the Cycladic islands and has thus been named Cycladic. It seems there were several Cycladic settlements. One of the most important, if not the most important, was located on the south coast, near the present village of Akroteri. This site favoured such an early settlement not only because it is situated in a sheltered region with safe anchorage for the boats of the period, but because it was ideal for the development of agriculture since it controlled the largest expanse of flat land on the island (ill. 9).

When, during the 2nd millennium B.C., the Minoan Civilisation spread out beyond the confines of Crete, the Cycladic islands, and in particular Santorini, accepted its influence most pronouncedly. Thus the Cycladic settlement of Akroteri was rapidly «Minoanised» and since it was situated directly opposite Crete it was not slow in developing into an important commercial habrour. This marked Minoan presence in Santorini is confirmed by the great prehistoric city which is coming to light in the excavations near the present-day Akroteri.

These excavations were begun in 1967 and continued intensively until the day of his death (1st October 1974) by Professor Spyridon Marinatos. He was attempting to prove an old theory of his — he had proposed it in 1939 — that the Santorini volcano was responsible for the decline of the Minoan Civilisation. Irrespective, however, of whether Marinatos' theory has been confirmed or not, it is a fact that this excavation has opened up a new chapter in the study of Aegean prehistory. The city which is now being revealed was covered beneath a thick layer of pumice and ash created by the eruption of the volcano in around 1500 B.C. The wonderful preservation of the monuments under this volcanic mantle enables the specialists to study better than ever all aspects of the life of the prehistoric inhabitants of Santorini. The town plan scarcely differs from that of the present-day villages of Santorini. Narrow cobbled streets traverse the settlement from one end to the other. Here and there they widen slightly to form squares. Under the paving of the streets runs the drainage system of the city which is connected directly to the plumbing in the houses. Waste water was conveyed into the sewers of the streets along round clay pipes. Houses stood on either side of the street, two, three and possibly four storeys

Plan of the upper storey of the West House. The walls of rooms 4
and 5 were decorated with wall-paintings.
(Plan Koumanoudis.)

high. Their walls were built of ordinary stones and mortar, frequently they were reinforced with wooden joists, a well-known anti-seismic system in Creto-Mycenaean architeceure. Large ashlared blocks were often used at the corners of the houses, as door and window frames, or to face entire façades of buildings (ill. 10, 11, 12). Impressive stone or wooden staircases connected the floors to each other (ill. 13). Small windows in the ground floors and large ones in the upper appartments ensured essential illumination and ventilation for the house. The ground floor or semi-basement rooms were used as magazines or workshops while the main residence was in the upper storeys. From the few casts which have been salvaged we know some of the more usual pieces of furniture in each house. Little tables, tripod, often with carved legs, small beds, stools and chairs, all fashioned from wood, they left their negatives in the fine volcanic ash. Also among the furniture of each house must be considered the loom installation. Even though we have no indication so far concerning its shape and size, it is certain that the loom was to be found in the upper storeys for the innumerable loom weights which constituted a part of its equipment have always been found here.

The mill installation is not absent from any house: a large stone consolidated on a built bench and other smaller stones at random all around for hand grinding. Inside the many pithoi which were stored in the magazines of each house have been found remains of pulses, flour, barley, almonds, dried fish etc. There are also pithoi which, as can be deduced from their shape, were used for the storage of oil, wine, olives et al. (ill. 14, 15, 16). It can be concluded from all this that each house was virtually self-sufficient in the essentials of life. Further information can be obtained concerning the economy of the island, as well as about the diet of its inhabitants. Apart from the above agricultural products, the animal bones which have been found in the excavation as food residues tell us about the significance of stock-raising in the economy of prehistoric Santorini. Sheep and goats occupy first place in animal husbandry and meat consumption. Pigs follow and last come the bovines which were probably reared for their milk and as beasts of burden rather than for their meat. Various types of sea-food, apart from fish (sea urchins, limpets, tritons) complete the diet of the inhabitants of prehistoric Akroteri.

However, the uniqueness of the Akroteri excavation is assured principally by the host of wall-paintings and their remarkably good state of preservation. There is hardly a house without at least one room decorated with wall-paintings. With one exception — Room Δ2 — all the wall-paintings have been found in rooms of the upper storey. Only the «Spring Fresco» was discovered in the ground-floor room Δ2.

On the smoothed plaster with which the inside walls of the houses are covered, the artist painted indifferent as to whether the plaster was wet or had dried. This is why in some places the technique of f r e s c o was applied and in others that of f r e s c o s e c c o or tempera. Finally, in other instances both techniques can be observed. The pigments are all mineral and it appears that some organic substance was used as a cohesive agent. Red, black, blue, orange and white are the colours one comes across in the Santorini wall-paintings.

Their subjects whether geometric or abstract motifs, whether idyllic landscapes or scenes from every - day life are always chosen in a way which meets the requirements of the space for which they were intended. The diversity of themes is so great and their presentation so rich that the wall-paintings, apart from their artistic merit, constitute a unique source of information about the society which created them. Occupations such as the collecting of crocus, or information pertaining to the costumes jewellery, male and female hairstyles, or the men's armour, the craft of ship-building and sailing are immediately made known through the wall-paintings. Every house in the Akroteri excavation constitutes a surprise. The West House with its varied and rich themes (ill. 17, 18, 19, 20, 21, 22, 23), Building Complex Δ with the excellence of the «Spring Fresco» in Δ2 (ill. 25, 27), Building B with the composition of monkeys in room B6 (ill. 31), the Antelopes and Boxing Children in room B1 (ill. 26, 28), the House of the Ladies with its homonymous compositions (ill. 30, 32) and the papyri (ill. 29) are all in an inferior position when compared with the totality of wall-paintings from Xeste 3 and Xeste 4 which are still in the stage of conservation and reconstruction.

Great too is the wealth of pottery from Akroteri. Apart from the thousands of every - day vessels (cooking pots, pithoi, amphorae, charcoal braziers et al.) there are vases which truly constitute household ornaments (ill. 33, 34). In both the painting and the pottery the elements of the Minoan civilisation are pronounced. And yet in both these areas the independence from the art of Crete is clearly apparent. The painting of Akroteri is freed from the artistic conventions of the Minoan palaces and is more like folk art. In the pottery also a similar independence is noticable. The number of vases which have been imported directly from Crete is quite small in comparison with the thousands of local production. Even the local vases which copy Minoan prototypes are distinguished by the diversity of decorative themes and the freedom in the arrangement of their decoration.

All this wealth which favoured the development of the arts cannot have been accrued from the agricultural activities of the prehistoric inhabitants of the island. Neither the size of Thera nor the variety of its

The island group of Thera and Therasia from an old map.

cultivation was sufficient to fulfill its needs and, at the same time, leave a surplus. On the other hand, even if the agricultural economy left a surplus it is not usual for an agricultural society to cultivate the arts. On the contrary, this mentality is more suited to a society of seafarers and merchants. And such, it seems, was the society of Akroteri. Indisputable evidence of this is the miniature fresco of the fleet from the West House (ill. 20, 21). From the excavation data so far it can be concluded that in prehistoric Akroteri there was apparently no absolute central authority. Both the architecture and distribution of wealth in the various house-holds confirm this assertion. A central executive did exist, however, for the society was well-organised. For example, a special service was required to maintain the drainage system in good order or to clear the rubble from the streets after an earthquake etc.

This organised society was surprised by the horrific eruption of the volcano in around 1500 B.C. The study of the stratigraphy above the ruins enables us to follow the various stages through which the eruption passed until the final destruction. It seems that the paroxysm began with slight earthquakes which warned the inhabitants of the disaster which followed. Neither skeletons nor valuable objects have been found buried beneath the ruins: the people took their precious possessions and fled. After the abandonment of the houses stronger earthquakes reduced many of them to ruins. A period of quiescence followed which gave the inhabitants the courage to return to their town. They began demolishing shaky walls, clearing the ruins to open the roads and repair the houses. During this phase the true eruption of the volcano commenced. Smoke and perhaps fumes warned the inhabitants for yet again they abandoned their homes, this time never to return. The enormous quantities of pumice and pozzuolana ejected by the volcano buried the whole island beneath a mantle which in some places exceeds 30 metres in depth. What happened to the inhabitants is completely unknown. Did they manage to embark on their boats and get away before the disaster happened? Did they drown in their boats, or did they remain on the island and were trapped beneath the pumice?

The material which erupted from the volcano and completely covered the island left an enormous void beneath the earth's crust. The roof of the chamber could not withstand for very long and it soon collapsed, fragmenting the island. The sea surged into the void thus created, surrounding the remnants of Thera and giving the islands of Santorini, Therasia and Aspronisi their present form. The area which was submerged was approximately 83 sq. kilometres, about four times greater than the area submerged in the eruption of Krakatoa with which the Santorini volcano is frequently compared. The bottom of this caldera, that is of the basin formed after the collapse of the roof of the volcano, in many cases achieves a depth of 400 metres beneath the surface of the sea.

The consequences of the eruption must have been tremendous, not only for Santorini, which literally disappeared, but also for the Aegean in general. Crete must certainly have suffered severe damage for it is situated only 60 miles to the south. Some scholars maintain that some of the events described in the Bible are directly related to the eruption of the Thera volcano. Thus the Plagues of the Pharaoh are interpreted as a result of the gases and dust which reached Egypt. The parting of the Red Sea is also explained by the tidal waves which the eruption generated. Only in this instance the mention of the Red Sea is considered to be a mistake instead of the Reed Sea which is located in the Port Said region (in Hebrew the phrases Red Sea and Reed Sea are phonetically very similar).

The destruction of Thera is also connected with the submergence of mythical Atlantis. The myth originates from Plato who, in two of his Dialogues — Timaios and Kritias — attempted to give the model of an ideally organised State. Many of the elements of the myth accord with reality as the archaeological pick-axe has revealed it. First of all the level of civilisation in Thera agrees with that of Atlantis. Large buildings built of red and white ashlared stones and decorated with wall-paintings, just like those described by Plato, have been discovered in Santorini. The period of time in which the civilisation of Atlantis is placed corresponds with the acme of the city of Akroteri. Finally, the manner in which the island of Santorini was submerged is reminiscent of the destruction of Atlantis. There are, however, serious objections to the identification of Santorini with the lost continent. The extent of Santorini in no way compares with the huge surface of Atlantis. The shape of the lost

The plain to the south-east of Akroteri, as seen from the village.

continent (consecutive rings of land and sea) can only be compared with the present form of Santorini. But this is a consequence of the eruption and submergence which took place in about 1500 B.C. The only great Mediterranean civilisation which can be connected with Atlantis is the Minoan civilisation of Crete. It is, however, impossible to regard Thera as the metropolis of the civilisation, as supporters of the theory relating it to Atlantis would wish. On Thera only a small phase of the final period — Late Minoan Ia — of the Minoan civilisation is represented and not all phases of its development. It seems, therefore, that Plato, presenting the paradigm of his ideal State, utilised information he had concerning the Minoan civilisation and the eruption of the Thera volcano which precipitated its end.

Tour of the Site

Before entering Telchines' Road; on the left is Xeste 3. A magnificent two-storey or three-storey building with impressive façades of ashlared stone. The large staircase as well as several rooms in the upper storey had monumental fresco compositions decorating their walls, such as the wall-painting with Women gathering Crocuses.

The southernmost section of Telchines' Road is surrounded by Building Γ to the left (west) and B to the right (east). The half-excavated building Γ has shown manifest indications that it was reused after the destruction but before the eruption. Its southernmost rooms Γ1 and Γ2 were used as workshops or store-rooms by the teams of workers who undertook the clearing of the ruins and freeing of the streets. Some of the many stone hammers and anvils found in this room are still 'in situ'. Building B is also half-excavated. Its eastern wing has suffered considerable damage from the torrent which passed this way before the

*Akroteri. From R. Zahn's excavation at the site
of Potamos at the end of the 19th century.
(Photograph of the German Archaeological Institute.)*

excavation began. The upper floors of rooms B1 and B6 had paintings on their walls. In B1 were the wall-paintings of the Antelopes and the Boxing Children, in B6 was the marvellous composition of Blue Monkeys.

After the small Square, Telchines' Road continues northwards. On the left (west) one can see the stratigraphy of the volcanic material and study the different phases of the eruption. On the right (east) extends the huge building complex Δ. It has five entrances, one on each of the sides, south, west and north and two on its eastern one. The present form of the building is a consequence of at least five different constructional phases. The south entrance leads into a room in which there is a mill installation $\Delta 15$ (for this reason the Square in front is called Mill Square). The

Akroteri. The village from the site of Potamos at the end of the 19th century. (Photograph of the German Archaeological Institute.)

adjacent room (Δ16) with a large window at street level was most probably a pottery shop. About four hundred vases were found, sorted according to quality, size and shape. The west entrance, which is protected by the Porch led to a staircase with wooden steps. The first

floor of room Δ1 with its p o l y t h y r o n must also have been an important chamber. Although accessible from the north entrance, Δ1 dominated the Triangle Square, thus named after its shape. The torrent which passed this way before the excavation started has destroyed a considerable part of the east wing of building complex Δ. Room Δ2 in this region is the only one in the entire excavation which had wall-paintings on the ground-floor. The "Spring Fresco" with the lilies and swallows was found 'in situ' protected beneath a thick layer of volcanic ash.

On the north-west side of Triangle Square stands the small two or three-storeyed West House. From the entrance which is located at the south-east corner of the house a staircase leads to the upper storeys. The most important sector was the west wing of the first floor with rooms 4a, 4 and 5. In room 4a there still exists today a perfect toilet installation. Room 4 was entirely covered with the wall-paintings of the little cabins (ikria) and room 5 was decorated with the wall-paintings of the two fishermen and the famous miniature frescoes of the fleet, the river etc.

From the Square in front of the north entrance of building complex Δ and northwards Telchines' Road has been destroyed by the torrent which also wrought serious damage to the eastern edge of the H o u s e o f t h e L a d i e s. Only a very few rooms of this house have been investigated. However, one of these produced the wonderful wall-paintings to which the whole house owes its name. Telchines' Road continued even further to the north and passed beside B u i l d i n g A which is also known as the Pithoi Magazine. Rooms A1, A2 and A3 were discovered full of pithoi which contained pulses, flour, barley etc.

The whole region east of the buildings in Telchines' Road remains, at the moment, uninvestigated. However, some buildings have already appeared. X e s t e 2 is a three-storeyed construction with a noteworthy system of wooden reinforcements on its north wall which has been revealed. It seems that the building Xeste 4, also three-storeyed, faced with white ashlar stones is also very important.

THE THERA EXHIBITION
IN THE NATIONAL ARCHAEOLOGICAL MUSEUM

In the Thera gallery of the National Museum an attempt is made to give as complete a picture of life in prehistoric Akroteri as possible. The photographic display shows only part of the efforts of Greek restorers, particularly in the field of wall-paintings, to recover the master-pieces of this unique art form and present them as complete as possible to public view. The rest of the exhibition consists of representative examples of every activity of the prehistoric inhabitants of Thera in around 1500 B.C.

The plaster-of-Paris cast found in the room of the Lilies (2) as well as a copy of it in wood and hide gives us an idea of the bed of the period. Stools, seats and small tripod tables complete the furniture of the house as corresponding plaster-of-Paris casts verify. The so-called "offering tables", of pottery or plaster, also in the exhibition, are miniatures of these tripod tables. Basketry was apparently an important activity in Akroteri for baskets were useful receptacles as they still are in the islands. Of the many remains of baskets which have been found in the excavation that on display is the best-preserved.

From the significant field of metal-working bronze vases and vessels (ewers, trays, frying pans and braziers) as well as tools (scales sickles, knives, nails etc.) indicate the great diversity in the use of metal. Lead was employed mainly for making weights for scales.

Stone tools and vessels, usually manufactured from hard stone of volcanic origin, constituted part of the every-day household objects. Oil lamps, mortars, grinders of such stones are to be seen in the exhibition showcases. Finer vases of better-quality stones (marble, alabaster, steatite, serpentine etc.) are displayed in the showcases outside the entrance to the exhibition (left).

Pottery, however, has left us more numerous examples than any other productive activity. From the thousands of vases and vessels the excavation has yielded, the vases in the exhibition constitute only a random sample. Beakers, ewers, cups, amphorae, cooking pots, plant pots, flower vases, strainers, braziers have been exhibited alongside other pottery objects (figurines, rhytons conical, zoomorphic and in the form of a lion's head). Through the vases which have been put on show an attempt has also been made to indicate the variety they exhibit from the point of view of decorative themes. Important pieces in this field are some sherds (pottery fragments) with representations of birds and animals, while much rarer are three sherds depicting human figures.

The showcase in the north-west corner of the exhibition is of especial interest. Various carbonised pulses, barley flour, snails, sea-urchin spines et al. are directly related to the diet of the prehistoric inhabitants of Akroteri and shed light on several aspects of the island's economy. Strainers, grills, tripod pottery "oven", mill-stones, mortars also found in the same showcase are indicative of the ways in which food was processed. Finally, the pottery vessel with handle and sooty lip must have been an oil lamp.

Gallery of Wall-paintings

Hundreds of square metres of wall-paintings have been found in Thera. Of these only the most representative and best-preserved have been displayed. The Antelopes and the Boxing Children originate from Room 1 in Building B (B1). From the same building (Room B6) come the Monkeys and the pieces depicting, perhaps, goats. The wall-painting

Akroteri. From R. Zahn's excavation at the site of Potamos.
(Photograph of the German Archaeological Institute.)

of the Lilies is the best-preserved piece and comes from Building Complex Δ (Room Δ 2). The so-called West House was particularly rich in wall-paintings as well as in diversity of subjects. The copy of the cabin which we see on the ships in the miniature wall-paintings, the Fisherman, the young "Priestess" as well as the frieze with the miniature representations of the ship-wreck, convoy of ships and the riparian landscape were all found in the West House. Finally, the large plants which some consider to be lilies and others to be papyrus were found in the House of the Ladies, a building which owes its name to the majestic ladies in their Minoan attire which we see in the corresponding wall-paintings.

*Akroteri. An oval utensil with decoration of dolphins. °"Kymbe".
(about 1500 B.C).*

*Akroteri. Table of offerings decorated with dolphin
(about 1500 B.C.*

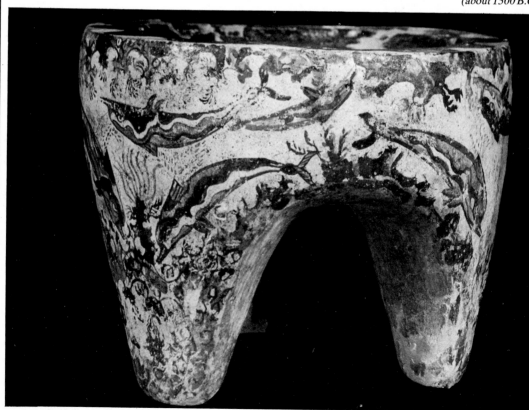

Nippled jug with flying swallows. Local matt-painted pottery
(about 1500 B.C.)

Akroteri. From the excavation of Telchnines' Street.

Akroteri. Eyed-jug of "marine style" with representation of dolphins
(about 1500 B.C.).

Akroteri. Spouted ewer with reed decoration from a local workshop
(about 1500 B.C.).

Akroteri. The Spring fresco (detail)
(about 1500 B.C.)

Akroteri. The room with the Spring fresco
(about 1500 B.C.)

LIST OF ILLUSTRATIONS

→

2. From Ormos (Bay), the old harbour of Santorini, one must climb up about six hundred steps in order to reach the capital, Phera.

1. Phera. Like most of the villages of Santorini, the capital resembles an eyrie on a rocky precipice.

About two million tons of pozzuolana go into the cement industry every year from the mines of Santorini.

4. The stepped road from the harbour to Phera.

Kato (Lower) Phera: A balcony overlooking the volcano.

Η ΑΝΑΛΗΨΙΣ ΤΟΥ ΧΡΙΣΤΟΥ

6. 7.8. Jewel of Kato Phera, the Church of Christos contains one of the marvels of folk wood-carving, its altar screen (templo) (7). Of the icons on the screen: The Ascension of Christ (6) and The Virgin and Child (8).

9. The Plain of Akroteri. Ideal site for the development of an important prehistoric settlement on the island. It lies just opposite Crete and its sea-shore is protected from the northerly winds.

Akroteri. The Triangular Square, an extension of Telchines' Road, is bounded to the north by the West House and to the south-east by building complex Δ.

11. Akroteri. The entrance to the West House. The windows beside and above the door ensure light for the straircase which leads to the upper storeys.

12. Akroteri. The western limit of the Triangular Square comprises a building of which only the façade has been revealed. To the west the porch of the west entrance to building complex Δ. Telchines' Road passes beneath this porch.

*13. Akroteri. From the north entrance to building
complex Δ, a stone staircase led directly to the
first floor.*

*14. Akroteri. Pithoi (storage jars) display
within the excavated are*

*15. Akroteri. Pithoi Magazine: Barley, flour,
pulses were among the contents of the pithoi.*

←

16. *Akroteri. Pithoi Magazine: Barley, flour, pulses were among*
    the contents of the pithoi.

18. *Akroteri. From the wall-paintings in the West House (room 5). On the sea shore scenes*
    following a sea battle and the disembarkation of warriors. High up in the background a
    pastoral scene.

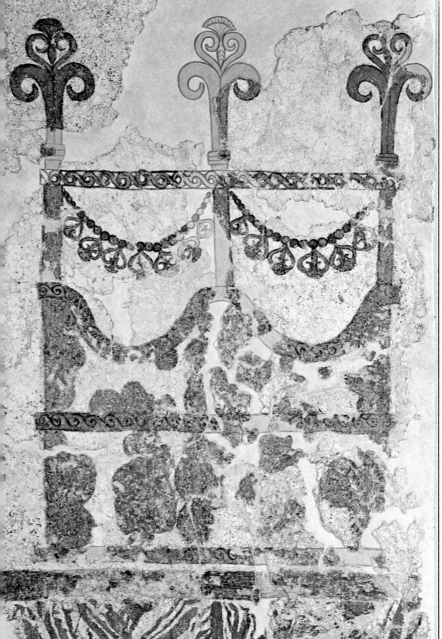

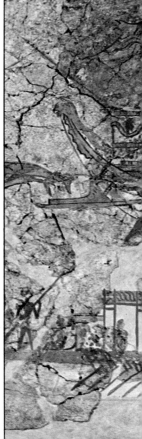

19. Akroteri. One of the seven painted cabins (ikria) which decorated Room 4 of the West House.

20. The miniature fresco of the escort of ships from Room 5 in the West House.

21. The «flagship» of the small fleet.

22. *Akroteri. The miniature fresco of the river from Room 5 of the West House.*

24. *Akroteri. From the miniature fresco of the river. A wild-cat prepares to pounce on the wild ducks which seem to have already realised this.*

23. Akroteri. The wall-painting of the young «Priestess» from the West House: she holds a brazier with glowing charcoal and sprinkles it with incense.

25. *Akroteri. The Lilies Fresco from Room Δ2. Swallows fly in daring formations among the blossoming lilies.*

26. *The wall-painting of the Boxing Children from Room B1.*

27. *Akroteri. Room Δ2. Detail from the Lilies Fresco.*